Transformative Choices: A Review Of 70 Years of FCC Decisions

Table of Contents

Introduction

This is a historical review of a series of pivotal decisions that helped shape today's communications landscape, including decisions by the FCC about the following: establishing commercial radio (by the Federal Radio Commission) in 1928; spectrum allocations and color standards for over-the air-television in 1945 and 1952; regulating cable television in 1966 and the early 1970s; authorizing customers in 1968 to attach equipment to their telephone lines; promoting direct broadcast satellites as a competitive alternative to cable television in 1982; letting the market decide the appropriate standards for digital cell phones in 1992; and adopting technical standards for high-definition and digital television in 1996 and 1997.

Overall, these decisions have been among the most critical the Commission has faced, generally involving the appearance of a new technology, communications device, or service. In many cases, the decisions involve spectrum allocation or usage. These are "transformative" decisions in the sense that they required the Commission to decide whether to "adopt, with minor revisions, the same legal and regulatory framework and mode of organization, or fundamentally transform them?"[1]

Some of the decisions are sufficiently far back in the past that policymakers may not be fully aware or have forgotten what was decided. In addition, these particular historical decisions happen also to shed light on topical issues. The Commission's choices about radio in the 1920s and television in the 1950s have their echoes in current debates about media concentration, diversity, and localism. Competing demands for scarce spectrum resonate from the earliest days to the present. The *Carterfone* decision can be seen as a precursor to open Internet principles. All these are reasons to study this history, even though policymakers no doubt will draw their own conclusions, and may even disagree, about the lessons to be learned from studying the past decisions.

From an academic perspective, too, these case studies offer an opportunity to examine a commonly-asserted view that regulatory policies throughout the economy underwent a major change in the 1970s, from protecting incumbents to promoting competition.[2] Is that general view reflected in FCC policies? Two case studies are relevant on this point: (1) the Commission's efforts to protect incumbents are shown in the cable industry case study; and (2) the Commission's efforts to promote entry by a new entrant are explored in the DBS study.

Finally, the case studies on digital cell phones and high-definition TV examine the Commission's role in setting technical standards, as well as the trade policy impact of these Commission decisions.

---

[1] Paul Starr, *The Creation of the Media* (2004) at 6.

[2] *See* Marc K. Landy and Martin A. Levin, "Creating Competitive Markets: The Politics of Market Design," in Marc K. Landy et al, *Creating Competitive Markets: The Politics of Regulatory Reform* (2007) ("A wave of deregulation hit aviation, trucking, and telecommunications in the mid-1970s, stimulated by an intellectually powerful and persuasive body of writings from experts in influential economics departments, law schools and think tanks.") at 2.

Radio (1928)

Commercial broadcasting began in 1920, when Westinghouse opened station KDKA and broadcast the November 2 election results.[3] For much of the rest of the decade, however, broadcasting was not a profitable operation and most broadcasters were not professional broadcasters, as we know them today.[4] Although large corporations like RCA, GE, AT&T, and Westinghouse dominated the manufacturing of radio sets and other aspects of the radio industry, by far the vast majority of broadcasters in the early 1920s were non-commercial entities: colleges and universities, labor unions, and civic organizations. Only 4.3% of all stations in 1926 were "commercial broadcasters."[5]

A major concern for industry leaders and policymakers was making broadcasters economically self-sufficient. In 1924, Secretary of Commerce Herbert Hoover, solicited major foundations to subsidize educational programming and proposed a 2% tax on sales of radio sets to "pay for daily programs of the best skill and talent."[6] Hoover also engaged in strenuous efforts to regulate the emerging radio industry but after a federal district court ruled that he lacked authority under the Radio Act of 1912 to issue broadcast licenses, took the decisive step of discontinuing all regulation.[7] Chaos ensued when more than 200 new broadcasters began to operate in the next six months. [See box]

Chaos in the airwaves

FRC Commissioner Orestes Caldwell explained in a June 1927 speech why the FRC needed to step in and assert control over the airwaves:

> "Proper separation between established stations was destroyed by other stations coming in and camping in the middle of any open spaces they could find, each interloper thus impairing reception of three stations—his own and two others. Instead of the necessary 50 kilocycle separation between stations in the same community, the condition soon developed where separations of 20 and 10 kilocycles, and even 8, 5, and 2, kilocycles existed. Under such separations, of course, stations were soon wildly blanketing each other and distracted listeners were assailed with scrambled programs."

Federal Radio Commission, *First Annual Report*, 1927, pp. 10-11.

Congress then enacted the Radio Act of 1927, establishing the Federal Radio Commission (FRC), to which it granted authority to issue licenses and regulations governing broadcasting.[8]

---

[3] Christopher H. Sterling, John Michael Kittross, *Stay Tuned: A History of American Broadcasting* (2002) at 66. The distinction of being the first broadcast station goes to KQW, licensed in 1912, but which began offering regularly scheduled news reports and music programs to San Jose listeners as early as 1909. Sterling and Kittross, *Stay Tuned* at 45. The station continues to operate today as KCBS in San Francisco. http://www.kcbs.com/pages/3504672.php. Network broadcasting started on January 4, 1923, when telephone circuits connected WNAC in Boston and WEAF in New York for a five-minute saxophone solo. Sterling and Kittross, *Stay Tuned* at 77.

[4] Robert McChesney, *Telecommunications, Mass Media, and Democracy: The Battle for Control of U.S. Broadcasting, 1928-1935 (Oxford University Press, 1994)* at 14.

[5] McChesney, *Telecommunications, Mass Media, and Democracy,* at 14-15. *But see* Sterling and Kittross, *Stay Tuned* at 70 (though non-commercial, many early broadcasters were often an arm of some other business or activity).

[6] McChesney, *Telecommunications, Mass Media, and Democracy,* at 16.

[7] Sterling and Kittross, *Stay Tuned* at 97-98.

[8] Sterling and Kittross, *Stay Tuned* at 141-143.

What did the FRC do?

The Federal Radio Commission created a new structure favoring commercial broadcasting. Specifically, the FRC:

-- adopted a series of orders widening the broadcast band to the entire spectrum between 550 kHz to 1500 kHz and removing portable stations from the air;[9]

-- allocated 40 nationwide high powered (generally 25,000-50,000 watts) "clear channels" on which only one station operated at nighttime, plus other regional and local channels;[10]

--set a preference for commercial use over stations representing religious, political, social, and economic viewpoints.[11]

The FRC's rationale for its actions

The main stated reason for regulating spectrum use was to bring order to the chaotic situation where stations operated without licenses and interference was a major concern.[12]

Though national networks could have been created by interconnecting (using telephone lines) a chain of lower-power local stations,

the FCC at that time favored networks consisting of high power, 'clear channels' that had nationwide coverage at nighttime.[13]

Commercial broadcasters pushed for national radio networks which they saw as "the only plan" for successfully financing radio broadcasting because it would permit the development of national advertising.[14]

The FRC initially steered away from endorsing these proposals to create a national advertiser-financed broadcasting system. The FRC's chief engineer described the channel allocation plan as entirely an engineering matter: "The reason for this is purely physical fact."[15] Indeed, the FRC stated in 1928 that its allocation plan was not intended for the primary benefit of advertisers.[16] By 1929, however, after having created 40 national clear channels and other regional high powered stations that depended on advertiser financing, the FRC acknowledged that the system it had created would need to be financed by

---

[9] Sterling and Kittross, *Stay Tuned* at 143.

[10] Federal Radio Commission, *General Order 40, First Annual Report* (1928) at 48-50.

[11] *In re Great Lakes Broadcasting Co.,* Federal Radio Commission, *Third Annual Report* (1929) at 32-35; Robert McChesney, *Telecommunications, Mass Media, and Democracy* at 26-28.

[12] For a different viewpoint, arguing that the private sector would have resolved interference issues though private arrangements with minimal governmental action, *see* John Berresford, *"How Government Can Bring New Communications to All Americans: Six Lessons of History,"* Program on Information Resources Policy, Harvard University (2004) at 24-28. Though interesting, this argument is ultimately unpersuasive because the private arrangements were too few and far between to solve a major nationwide problem.

---

[13] Nationwide coverge at nighttime is possible for AM radio stations due to a phenomenon called "skywave" propagation. To prevent massive interference, the small number of clear channel stations was granted nighttime exclusivity. Since 1980, however, these stations (now called Class A stations) generally broadcast over a 750 mile range, rather than nationally. http://www.fcc.gov/mb/audio/bickel/daytime.html.

[14] McChesney, *Telecommunications, Mass Media, and Democracy,* at 23.

[15] Critics questioned the FRC's claims. *See* McChesney, *Telecommunications, Mass Media, and Democracy,* at 22 (noting that the engineer was an employee of the affected industries and returned to his corporate employment after his FRC service ended). *See also* Thomas Streeter, *Selling the Air: A Critique of the Policy of Commercial Broadcasting in the United States* (1996) at 100 (disputing FCC impartiality).

[16] McChesney, *Telecommunications, Mass Media, and Democracy,* at 25 (noting FRC statement that "advertising is usually offensive to the listening public.").

advertising: "without advertising, broadcast would not exist."[17]

The FRC also said it was driven by spectrum scarcity to favor "general purpose" commercial stations over the non-profit ("propaganda") stations. In regard to "propaganda" stations, the FRC stated:

> "There is not room in the broadcast band for every school of thought, religious, political, social, and economic, each to have its separate broadcasting station, its mouthpiece in the ether."[18]

In practice, the FRC issued licenses to well-financed commercial stations rather than to non-commercial stations.[19]

Impact of the decision: the long view

* The FRC's decisions brought an end to the chaos in the airwaves that had existed in the mid-1920s and set the structure of the broadcasting industry for decades.[20]

* Commercial broadcasting replaced non-commercial broadcasting as the dominant force in radio.[21] [See box.]

* National radio networks rose in prominence. In 1926, the National Broadcasting Company (NBC) was created, with 22 affiliates. This became known as the

---

> **The decline of non-commercial radio**
>
> "Although more than 200 educational AM stations had been started in the early 1920s, almost all of them left the air by the end of the decade."
> Sterling, and Kittross, *Stay Tuned*, at 115-116, 124-127.
>
> "Nonprofit broadcasting accounted for only 2 percent" of all air time by 1934.
> McChesney, *Telecommunications, Mass Media, and Democracy*, at 30 -31).

Red network. NBC's second network, known as the Blue network, had 6 affiliates. These added up to 7 percent of all stations.

By 1933, Red had 28, Blue had 24, and 36 were supplemental, for a total of 88 NBC affiliates, nearly 15 percent of all affiliates. The Columbia Broadcasting System (CBS) had 17 affiliates in 1928 (4 percent of the total) and rose to 91 affiliates in 1933 (16 percent of the total).[22] More significantly, NBC and CBS were affiliated with all but 3 of the 40 "clear channels" and accounted for 97 percent of nighttime broadcasting (when the smaller stations were not allowed to operate).[23]

* Advertising became the principal source of broadcasting revenue. Radio advertising, a marginal factor in 1927, rose to $100 million in 1930.[24] Radio stations' income rose from less than $5 million in 1927 to $56 million four years later.[25]

---

[17] *In re Great Lakes Broadcasting Co.,* Federal Radio Commission, *Third Annual Report* at 35. *See* McChesney, *Telecommunications, Mass Media, and Democracy,* at 25.
[18] *In re Great Lakes Broadcasting Co.,* Federal Radio Commission, Federal Radio Commission, *Third Annual Report* at 34..
[19] *See* McChesney, *Telecommunications, Mass Media, and Democracy,* at 26-28 ("by the FRC's interpretation, commercial advertising is deemed the *only* legitimate form of financial support for a broadcaster, as by definition any other form of support had propaganda strings attached.").
[20] Sterling, and Kittross, *Stay Tuned,* at 150-151.
[21] *See* Streeter, *Selling the Air,* at 99; McChesney, *Telecommunications, Mass Media, and Democracy,* at 28.

---

[22] Sterling, and Kittross, *Stay Tuned,* at 117-122.
[23] McChesney, *Telecommunications, Mass Media, and Democracy,* at 29. The average independent station had 566 watts of power, and the average NBC station over 10,000 watts. *Id.*
[24] McChesney, *Telecommunications, Mass Media, and Democracy,* at 30. *See* Streeter, *Selling the Air,* at 98 ("By 1933, broadcast entertainment delivered by networks and saturated with advertising was already a fixture of American culture.").
[25] Sterling, and Kittross, *Stay Tuned,* at 127.

Broadcast Television (1945, 1952)

In the postwar period, television stations were on the air in only six cities (New York, Washington, Schenectady, Chicago, Philadelphia, and Los Angeles) and broadcasting only a few hours a day. Demand grew quickly, so that by 1948 there were 34 stations in 21 cities, and over a million TV sets. [26] Television had arrived, and the FCC faced a series of pivotal decisions that helped to shape its future. They involved resolving competing claims for spectrum for TV and FM radio; whether to use the VHF or UHF bands; adopting a color TV standard, and deciding whether to establish educational TV (later known as "public television"). The FCC's options were:

i. Permit FM radio to retain its VHF channels and assign TV channels in the UHF band (which could accommodate the wider 16 MHz channels CBS requested) after the new technical standards were set; *or*
 Move FM radio to an upper part of the VHF band and allocate TV channels in the VHF band, delaying a decision on color TV, high-definition TV and UHF allocations for TV.

ii. In interpreting section 307(b) of the Communications Act, which required the FCC to distribute licenses on a "fair, efficient, and equitable" basis to all States and localities, [27] choose between assigning licenses on a local or regional basis.

iii. Allocate space for educational TV [ETV] in the VHF or UHF bands or, alternatively,

leave it to commercial broadcasters to produce educational content.

iv. Choose between the color standard proposed by CBS or RCA.

Stakeholders

There were two competitors for VHF channels: <u>FM radio</u> (esp. radio pioneer Edwin Armstrong) wanted to keep and expand on its 55 channels in the 42-50 MHz band; <u>commercial TV networks</u> (esp. RCA) wanted the VHF channels for television.

<u>RCA</u>, as the leading provider of black and white TV sets and TV programming, also favored continuing TV in black and white on 6 MHz standard channels but <u>CBS</u>, the disruptive new entrant, urged delaying TV allocations until after deciding on color and high-definition standards.

What did the FCC do?

-- In 1945, the FCC moved FM radio up the VHF band, from 42-50 MHz to 88-108 MHz (1945); [28]

-- At the same time, the FCC also rejected proposals for wideband, high-definition color TV on the UHF band and instead allocated 12 channels (2 to 13) in the VHF band for TV, with channels 2-6 at 54 MHz to 88 MHz, and channels 7-13 at 174 MHz to 216 MHz.; [29]

--In 1948, with 50 stations on the air, and an additional 50 construction permits issued, the FCC instituted a "freeze" on licenses. [30]

-- In 1952, the FCC added 70 UHF channels (14 to 83) for commercial and non-commercial TV, intending the VHF and

---

[26] Sterling and Kittross, *Stay Tuned,* at 251, 278. The FCC allocated 19 VHF channels in 1937 for experimental TV and 18 VHF channels in 1941 for commercial TV (though most of the channels were used by the military during the war).
[27] *Sixth R& O* at ¶¶ 12-18, in Pike and Fisher, *Radio Regulation*, Vol. 1, Part 3, at 91:603-91:606.

[28] Sterling and Kittross, *Stay Tuned,* 249-253.
[29] Sterling and Kittross, *Stay Tuned,* 251.
[30] Sterling and Kittross, *Stay Tuned,* at 319-321.

UHF stations to "constitute an integral part of a single, nationwide television service";[31]

-- The FCC also assigned local, not regional or national TV licenses;[32]

--Reserved one VHF channel for educational broadcasting in any city with more than 3 VHF channels (unless all the VHF channels had already been assigned), and one UHF channel in other cities.[33]

Initially, the FCC picked the CBS color standard (1950) but later reversed itself and adopted the NTSC standard developed by RCA (1953).[34]

The FCC's rationale for its actions

FM radio v. TV: Initially, in 1940, the FCC, under new Chairman James Lawrence Fly, favored FM, primarily to limit the dominant power of radio giants, RCA and NBC. Thus, the FCC transferred a TV channel (44 to 50 MHz) to FM radio, giving FM a total of 40 channels in which to expand.[35] However, after Fly left office in 1944, FM lost ground. Faced with competing demands for the same spectrum band, the FCC picked TV over FM radio, and justified its decision in part on an engineering analysis (later alleged to be flawed) predicting that FM radio would experience interference from the sunspot

cycle in 1947-1948.[36] The FCC's 1945 decision was a compromise decision, intended to accommodate the competing demands of multiple parties (FM v. TV, RCA v. CBS, etc.), but RCA proved to be too tenacious to lose.[37]

TV allocations: The FCC reasoned, in 1945, that there was not enough capacity in the VHF band to provide the 30 or more channels needed to provide nationwide, competitive television broadcasting, so it allocated 12 channels in the VHF band for TV, authorized experimental use on a limited scale in the UHF band (between 480 and 920 MHz), and suggested it would find more space for TV in the UHF band later.[38]

---

[31] Television Allocations, *Sixth Report & Order,* at ¶¶ 22-25, 197 in Pike and Fisher, *Radio Regulation,* Vol. 1, Part 3, at 91:607-608, 664 (1952).
[32] Television Allocations, *Sixth Report & Order,* at ¶¶ 70-79 in Pike and Fisher, *Radio Regulation,* Vol. 1, Part 3, at 91:622-624. *See* Roger Noll, Merton Peck, and John J. McGowan, *Economic Aspects of Television Regulation,* (1973) at 100-101.
[33] Sterling and Kittross, *Stay Tuned,* at 328.
[34] Sterling and Kittross, *Stay Tuned,* at 322-324; Carl Shapiro and Hal R. Varian, *Information Rules* (1999), at 214-218.
[35] Hugh R. Slotten, *Radio and Television Regulation, Broadcast Technology in the United States, 1920-1960* (2000), at 118.

---

[36] Sterling and Kittross, *Stay Tuned,* at 252 (noting "flawed" prediction of former FCC engineer that FM radio would experience interference in the 40 to 50 MHz band when the 11-year sunspot cycle reached its peak in 1947-1948). *See also* Slotten, *Radio and Television Regulation,* at 126 ("controversial" evidence). Dale Hatfield, a respected technology expert and former Chief of the FCC's Office of Engineering and Technology (1997-2000), supports the original findings: "In my opinion, if the FM band had been left in the 42-50 MHz range, we would, in fact, be suffering from rather severe interference during periods of high solar activity even today. In fact, recent experience with the DTV transition supports that argument. Television stations making the transition have almost without exception tried to avoid operation on TV Channel 2 (54-60 MHz) and the low VHF channels more generally because of interference." *Email communication with Dale Hatfield, March 21, 2010.*
[37] Slotten, *Radio and Television Regulation,* at 127; Sterling and Kittross, *Stay Tuned,* at 252.
[38] *FCC Chairman Coy,* on September 13, 1948, said:

> "These [12 VHF channels] were not intended to represent a satisfaction of television's requirement; 12 simply represented the most VHF spectrum space—72 [MHz]—which, on a relative basis, the Commission then believed was justifiable for a wide-band service whose full accommodation obviously would have to be higher in the spectrum."

The FCC most likely found it difficult to delay allocating channel capacity until color standards were set and HDTV developed (as CBS had proposed), because that would have run counter to the post-WWII pressure from consumers and industry to produce consumer goods immediately.[39]

Because demand for channels increased, the FCC, in 1952, allocated additional capacity for television in the UHF band, but did not, as it had earlier suggested, move all TV service to UHF, most likely because of resistance from incumbent operators in the VHF band who had large investments in VHF transmitters and receivers.[40]

"Intermixing" (i.e., assigning VHF and UHF stations to compete in the same communities) was doomed to fail because the new UHF stations in many cities were forced to compete with existing VHF stations whose customers already owned VHF-only receivers and were unlikely to incur the additional expense and inconvenience of buying, installing and operating a UHF tuner that down-converted the UHF channels to VHF. The FCC noted that intermixing may "temporarily handicap operations in the new UHF band and place certain communities at a disadvantage," but remained hopeful that solutions would be worked out in the long run.[41] But, no solution emerged until Congress passed the All-Receiver Act in 1962, mandating that all receivers must be able to receive both VHF and UHF signals.[42]

Local or regional licenses: Under the regional station concept, as proposed by Dumont Broadcasting, regional stations with powerful transmitters could serve a large area and provide most of the country with as many as seven networks. The FCC instead preferred to license less-powerful local stations that would permit local communities to have their own stations but would reduce the number of channels any viewer would receive.[43]

Educational broadcasting: Commercial broadcasters opposed reserving channels for educational TV, arguing that educational broadcasters did not have the resources to offer TV programming and would not be able to use the channels they were seeking. The FCC, led by Commissioner Frieda Hennock (the first female Commissioner), disagreed. Instead, the FCC ruled that when more than three VHF channels were assigned to a city, one would be for education. Additional VHF channels were reserved for educational institutions. [By 2001, these had grown to more than 370 public TV stations.][44]

Color standard: The FCC initially favored CBS' color standard over RCA's because it was technically superior, even though a significant drawback was that CBS's color sets were not backward compatible with existing black and white sets.[45] After consumers failed to buy CBS color sets, the FCC agreed to change the color standard to the industry consensus NTSC standard.[46]

---

[39] Sterling and Kittross, *Stay Tuned,* at 254-255.
[40] Sterling and Kittross, *Stay Tuned,* at 325-326.
[41] *Sixth R& O* at ¶ 199, Pike and Fisher, *Radio Regulation*, Vol. 1, Part 3, at 91:665 (1952); Sterling and Kittross, at 387-388.
[42] Sterling and Kittross, *Stay Tuned,* at 415-416.
[43] Noll *et al*, *Economic Aspects of Television Regulation,* at 101.
[44] Sterling, and Kittross, *Stay Tuned,* at 328; *Sixth R& O* at ¶ 38, in Pike and Fisher, *Radio Regulation*, Vol. 1, Part 3, at 91:612-91:613 (1952).
[45] Sterling and Kittross, *Stay Tuned,* at 322-324; Shapiro and Varian, *Information Rules,* at 214-218. David Sarnoff, RCA's chief, acknowledged after a test that RCA's color was not that good: "The monkeys were green, the bananas were blue, and everyone had a good laugh." Shapiro and Varian, *Information Rules,* at 215.
[46] Shapiro and Varian, *Information Rules,* at 215-216.

Impact of the decisions: the long view

FM radio: Though FM radio gained by getting more channels, the creator of FM radio, Edwin Armstrong, lost, as the FCC decision rendered obsolete 400,000-500,000 radio sets.[47] In 1941, FM radio seemed to be on the march, with 67 commercial FM stations (and another 43 license applications pending at the FCC), but the FCC's 1945 allocation stopped FM in its tracks.[48] FM radio did not start to grow again until the 1960s.[49]

"Mess in the Making"

"It would be hard to overemphasize the importance of the 1945 decisions that stemmed from these hearings. Much of their structure remains, and they are the source of many of today's problems."

Sterling and Kittross, *Stay Tuned,* at 255, 319.

TV allocations: The 1945 and 1952 allocations decisions created problems that plagued the FCC for decades.[50] Because the FCC had not allocated sufficient spectrum for TV to satisfy the post-war needs in 1945, FCC engineers struggled for years to meet demand by narrowing mileage separations between stations until reception was impossible in many areas, leading broadcasters and viewers to complain.

* Even greater problems resulted from the 1952 decision to intermix VHF and UHF. With VHF sets already in use, and manufacturers uninterested in producing sets that received both VHF and UHF signals, UHF stations were at a disadvantage. By 1958, only 308 communities out of 1275 had stations in operation and in larger markets "virtually no UHF station was doing well" against a VHF competitor.[51]

* Though television was almost universal in the United States by the early 1960s, viewers did not receive anywhere near the amount of competitive choice the FCC had expected from its earlier decisions. Overall, the result for most Americans was fewer on-air stations, more oligopolies, and higher advertising costs than intended.[52]

Color standard: The networks invested heavily in color transmission equipment, with the result that, by 1957, 106 of 158 stations in the top 40 cities had the ability to transmit in color, but viewers stayed away: Only 3 percent of households had color TV sets in 1963. Color TV did not take hold until the mid-1960s, after prices of sets fell and sufficient content was produced to make color TV attractive to consumers.[53]

Local or regional licenses: By focusing on localism as a principal goal, and by intermixing VHF and UHF stations, the FCC missed the chance to create as many as 7 national networks.[54] If the FCC had adopted the concept of "regional TV stations centered around powerful transmitters receivable over a large area," most of the country could have had as many as seven VHF channels.[55]

---

[47] Sterling and Kittross, *Stay Tuned,* at 253 (400,000); Slotten, *Radio and Television Regulation,* at 119 (500,000).
[48] Slotten, *Radio and Television Regulation,* at 118.
[49] Sterling and Kittross, *Stay Tuned,* at 249-253, 389, 412-415.
[50] *See e.g.,* Sterling and Kittross, *Stay Tuned,* at 255, 319 ("Mess in the Making: 1945 through 1948"), 387-391 ("The UHF Mess").

[51] Sterling and Kittross, *Stay Tuned,* at 387-388, 415-416 (Between 1952 and 1959, 55% of 165 UHF stations that went on the air shut down.)
[52] Sterling and Kittross, *Stay Tuned,* at 331.
[53] Shapiro and Varian, *Information Rules,* at 216.
[54] Noll *et al, Economic Aspects of Television Regulation,* at 99-120, esp. 116.
[55] Noll *et al, Economic Aspects of Television Regulation,* at 101.

Instead, because licenses were issued for local stations, a different result followed:

"The local station concept, on the other hand, would reduce the power of each station, permitting many more communities to have their own station but reducing the number of channels any given viewer would receive."[56]

As a result of favoring local stations over regional stations, only the "Big 3" national networks developed in the U.S., until 1987,[57] when a fourth (Fox) was added.[58] In effect, localism triumphed at the expense of competition.[59] But, "localism" has not produced the desired local programming. As a leading economics text written in 1973 noted:

"the fact remains that almost all of the programming broadcast over the local stations has a national focus. The network affiliates, which constitute the vast majority of VHF stations, rely on the networks for 82 percent of their prime-time programming. Of the remaining 18 percent, a high proportion is devoted to non-network films and other programming. Outside of prime time, the reliance is less—particularly for affiliates of ABC, which offers less daytime network programming—but the pattern is much the same. Few local programs other than local news and weather and sports are offered."[60]

Clearly, the lack of local programming was a concern for Congress and the FCC, who expected a much more extensive role for local broadcasting than turned out to be the case. [See box]

---

[56] Noll *et al*, *Economic Aspects of Television Regulation,* at 101.

[57] *See* Stanly M. Besen, Thomas G. Krattenmaker, A. Richard Metzger, Jr., and John R. Woodbury, *Misregulating Television* (1984) ("a confluence of avoidable FCC policy choice-…virtually assured that only three, national, full-scale television networks would succeed.").

[58] Florence Setzer and Jonathan Levy, *"Broadcast Television in a Multichannel Marketplace,"* OPP Working Paper Series (FCC, June 1991) (Fox began service in the 1987/1988 season, distributing programming five nights a week to independent stations) at 28, n.25.

[59] Noll *et al*, *Economic Aspects of Television Regulation,* at 101.

[60] Noll *et al*, *Economic Aspects of Television Regulation,* at 108-109.

Cable Television (1966, 1970s)

From its modest beginnings around 1950, cable TV grew rapidly as an alternative distribution mechanism to broadcast TV. [61] In the 1950s, new cable systems were introduced at an annual rate of 24.9 percent and subscriber growth was about 40 percent annually. In 1959, the FCC adopted a policy supporting the growth of cable TV, except in the extreme case in which a broadcaster could show that "it was the only local broadcast service whose existence was threatened."[62] By 1966, more than 1 million homes out of 60 million received cable, and more than 1,200 systems were operating.[63] By then, the FCC began to change its view that cable was no longer a threat to broadcasting.

What did the FCC do?

1966: The FCC decided to limit and regulate the manner in which CATV competes with the basic off-air television broadcast service.[64] Specifically, the FCC imposed two conditions on cable systems: (1) the cable system must carry the signals of all local stations ["must carry"], and (2) the cable system was not permitted to carry the programs of a distant station when they duplicated the programs of a local station fifteen days before or after the local broadcast.[65] Most significantly, the FCC broadened the scope of its concern from markets in which the broadcaster was the only TV station to the top 100 markets.[66]

1972: The FCC adopted complex rules (described by two scholars as "baroque"):[67]

* "Must carry" was still required;
* The number of distant signals that could be imported (e.g., 3 networks, 3 independents) varied depending on the stations market size (top 50, 50-100, smaller markets);
* Cable operators could not "leapfrog" nearby stations in favor of large-market independent stations;
* Syndicated network programming on local stations was protected from competition by identical programming on imported signals;
* Systems with 3,500 or more subscribers had to originate some of their own programming;
* Channels had to be set aside for public, educational, and government use;
* Channel capacity had to be added if all channels were in use for more than 80 percent of the time in any three hour period for six weeks.[68]

From 1974-1978, the FCC undid the 1972 rules. First, in 1974, the FCC allowed cable systems to import unlimited signals during a

---

[61] The first subscription cable system was established in Lansford, Pennsylvania, in 1950, though non-commercial systems existed a few years earlier in Pennsylvania and Oregon. *See* Robert W. Crandall and Harold Furchtgott-Roth, *Cable Television: Regulation or Competition* (1996) at 3.

[62] *See* Stanley M. Besen and Robert W. Crandall, "The Deregulation of Cable Television," 44 *Law and Contemporary Problems* 77 (1981), at 83.

[63] Gregory S. Crawford, "Cable Regulation in the Satellite Era," (2006), at 5-6, http://www.u.arizona.edu/~gsc818/research/papers/cablereg.pdf. *See* Sterling and Kittross, *Stay Tuned,* at 417.

[64] Rules and Regulations Relating to the Distribution of Television Broadcast Signals by the Community Antenna Television Systems, *Second Report and Order,* 2 FCC 2d 725 (1966). *See* Besen *et al*," The Deregulation of Cable Television," 44 *Law and Contemporary Problems* at 88. Though the Commission never considered this option, the FCC instead could have restricted broadcast TV to permit cable to emerge as a strong competitor.

[65] *Second Report and Order,* 2 FCC 2d at 747-756.

[66] *Second Report and Order,* 2 FCC 2d at 783.

[67] Besen *et al*," The Deregulation of Cable Television," 44 *Law and Contemporary Problems* at 95.

[68] Besen *et al*," The Deregulation of Cable Television," 44 *Law and Contemporary Problems* at 95-96, *especially* Table II.

A postscript is worth noting: as cable TV grew and prospered and demonstrated market power from its monopoly position in some communities, Congress, the FCC, and local jurisdictions responded by imposing rate regulation and other restrictions.[70]

The FCC's rationale for its actions

The FCC's actions in 1966 were designed to prevent "unfair" competition by cable systems and to foreclose any "adverse impact" on broadcasting as a result of cable's growth.[71]

The purpose of extending these rules to the top 100 markets was to protect UHF broadcasters, who were still struggling to gain a foothold despite the FCC's efforts since the 1950s to promote broadcasting in the UHF band.[72]

The complex 1972 rules were the result of a compromise between the broadcasters and cable operators that was defended by the FCC as being in the public interest because they protected local broadcasting while allowing some growth for cable.[73]

period in which local stations were not broadcasting. Leapfrogging restrictions were abandoned in 1976. In 1977, cable operators were permitted to use 4.5 meter receive-only earth stations, which drastically cut their costs and made pay-cable affordable. In 1978, the Commission exempted smaller systems from all exclusivity and signal-carriage rules.[69]

---

[69] Besen *et al*," The Deregulation of Cable Television," 44 *Law and Contemporary Problems,* at 99-100.

---

[70] Sterling and Kittross, *Stay Tuned,* at 417-418; Crawford, "Cable Regulation in the Satellite Era," at 6-11.
[71] Besen *et al*," The Deregulation of Cable Television," 44 *Law and Contemporary Problems,* at 88. *See* Crandall and Furchtgott-Roth, *Cable Television: Regulation or Competition,* at 3 ("high-water mark of repressive regulation").
[72] Community Antenna Television Systems, *Second Report and Order,* 2 FCC 2d at 781: *See also* Besen *et al*," The Deregulation of Cable Television," 44 *Law and Contemporary Problems,* at 89.
[73] Crandall and Furchtgott-Roth, *Cable Television: Regulation or Competition,* at 4. *See also* Besen *et al*," The Deregulation of Cable Television," 44 *Law and Contemporary Problems,* at 97 ("The obvious intent of the rules was to continue to protect large-market broadcasters while unburdening cable somewhat.").

Impact of the decision: the long view

The mid-1970s proved to be a decisive decade in the twists and turns of FCC's regulation of the cable industry.[74] First, there was a decisive shift in regulatory thinking in favor of a "policy which would permit some cable growth in major markets."[75]

Second, economic studies began to show that the growth of the cable industry might actually benefit—rather than harm—broadcasters, particularly owners of UHF stations who would be better able to compete with VHF stations in homes served by cable.[76] Finally, cable grew in influence as the industry passed the 5 million subscriber mark in 1971 "with no demonstrable harm to broadcasters."[77]

The deregulatory efforts of 1974-1978 had a dramatic impact:

> "As the 1980s dawned, therefore, cable was free of the most repressive federal regulatory provisions that had limited its ability to offer diverse programming, but it was still subject to regulation by municipal or state franchising or regulatory efforts."[78]

Adding to the deregulatory efforts, the FCC's Open Skies policies led to competition in the domestic satellite field that made low-cost satellite transmission an attractive alternate to the more expensive terrestrial microwave networks that had been the principal means of distributing video programming to cable and broadcast stations.[79]

Cable deregulation also got a significant boost from the court decision in *Home Box Office v. FCC* (1977), which rejected the FCC's claim of jurisdiction on the theory that cable was subject to regulation because it impinged upon the FCC's primary responsibility over local broadcasting. The FCC did not attempt to rewrite the rules, thus leaving cable networks free to use satellite as a means of nationally distributing programming.[80]

Meanwhile, broadcast TV in the UHF band never grew as much as the FCC hoped. By 1976, of 590 commercial UHF assignments, nearly 400 were still vacant.[81]

---

[74] Sterling and Kittross, Stay Tuned, at 468 ("Over nearly four decades, the FCC's regulation of cable television has undergone substantial changes in direction."). *See generally,* Daniel Brenner et al, Cable Television and Other Nonbroadcast Video: Law and Policy (2004) at 2-10 to 2-22 (discussing the 1992 Cable Act and its precedents).

[75] Besen *et al,*" The Deregulation of Cable Television," 44 *Law and Contemporary Problems,* at 96 (citing in particular the role of a new FCC Chairman, Dean Burch, and the influence of the Office of Telecommunications Policy).

[76] Besen *et al,*" The Deregulation of Cable Television," 44 *Law and Contemporary Problems,* at 97 (citing in particular studies by the Rand Corporation).

[77] Besen *et al,*" The Deregulation of Cable Television," 44 *Law and Contemporary Problems,* at 97. By 1976, 1 of every 6 homes subscribed to cable, and there were more than 3,700 systems. Sterling and Kittross, *Stay Tuned,* at 417.

[78] Crandall and Furchtgott-Roth, *Cable Television: Regulation or Competition,* at 4.

[79] Crandall and Furchtgott-Roth, *Cable Television: Regulation or Competition,* at 5-6. *See also* Besen *et al,*" The Deregulation of Cable Television," 44 *Law and Contemporary Problems,* at 108, *citing* FCC Network Inquiry Staff, *Video Interconnection: Cost and Regulatory Policies (March, 1980)* at 68-73.

[80] *See* Streeter, *Selling the Air,* at 177, n.21; Crandall and Furchtgott-Roth, *Cable Television: Regulation or Competition,* at 6.

[81] Sterling and Kittross, *Stay Tuned,* at 415-416.

Carterfone (1968)

In the 1940's and 1950's, the FCC had repeatedly supported prohibitions against any "foreign attachments," e.g., the Jordaphone (a prototype of today's answering machine) and the Hush-A-Phone (a small plastic device snapped onto the mouthpiece to provide privacy in crowded office environments).[82] The Court of Appeals reversed the FCC's Hush-A-Phone decision, stating: "The mere fact that the telephone companies can provide a rival device would seem a poor reason for disregarding Hush-A-Phone's value in assuring a quiet line."[83] Next up was the Carterfone, a device that linked mobile radio to the landline network.[84] From 1959 to

1966, Carter Electronics had produced 4500 of these devices and sold 3500 devices to dealers. AT&T filed tariffs prohibiting their use.

What did the FCC do?

In 1968, the FCC struck down AT&T's tariff and ordered all carriers to file new tariffs permitting use of devices not made by the phone companies.[85] The FCC found that AT&T's tariff was unreasonable because it would have prohibited the Carterfone attachment whether or not it harmed the telephone system: "the vice of the present tariff … is that it prohibits the use of harmless as well as harmful devices."[86]

The FCC also found that the tariff was discriminatory because it permitted customers to attach equipment similar to the Carterfone provided that the equipment was manufactured by AT&T.[87]

On reconsideration, the FCC set some limits, insisting that it was not "opening the door to customer ownership of telephone handsets."[88]

Impact of the decision: the long view

Although the FCC's decision allowed users to connect equipment to the telephone line, AT&T filed a revised tariff that also permitted the use of privately supplied telephones and other telephone equipment. As a former FCC Commissioner later noted:

> *Carterfone* had said nothing about substitute equipment; there is no indication that the FCC intended to terminate AT&T's monopoly on non-peripheral terminal equipment."[89]

---

[82] A casebook describes the FCC's Hush-A-Phone decision as: "Perhaps [the FCC's] most comical order, revealing how a regulatory mind-set can sometimes overwhelm common sense." Michael K. Kellogg, John Thorne, and Peter W. Huber, *Federal Telecommunications Law* (1992) at 502.

[83] *Hush-A-Phone v. United States*, 238 F. 2d266 (D.C.Cir. 1956).

[84] The device in question was the Carterfone, described by the FCC as follows:

> "The Carterfone is designed to be connected to a two-way radio at the base station serving a mobile radio system. When callers on the radio and on the telephone are both in contact with the base station operator, the handset of the operator's telephone is placed on a cradle in the Carterfone device. A voice control circuit in the Carterfone automatically switches on the radio transmitter when the telephone caller is speaking; when he stops speaking, the radio returns to a receiving condition. A separate speaker is attached to the Carterfone to allow the base station operator to monitor the conversation, adjust the voice volume, and hang up his telephone when the conversation has ended."

Use of the Carterfone Device in Message Toll Telephone Prices, 13 FCC Rcd 420, *recon. denied*, 14 FCC 2d 571, 572 (1968).

[85] *Carterfone*, 13 FCC 2d at 423.

[86] *Carterfone*, 13 FCC2d at 424.

[87] *Carterfone*, 13 FCC2d at 423-424.

[88] *Carterfone*, 14 FCC2d at 572. *See* Kellogg, *et al, Federal Telecommunications Law*, at 504.

[89] *See* Glen O. Robinson, "The Titanic Remembered: AT&T and the Changing World of Telecommunications," 5 *Yale Journal of*

Two additional steps needed to be taken for the full impact of *Carterfone* to be realized. First, in 1975, the FCC created the Part 68 rules which required that all terminal equipment connect to the network through standard plugs and jacks. Any manufacturer that met the Part 68 standards was authorized to produce customer premises equipment [CPE].[90]

Second, in the *Computer Inquiries* (decided in the 1970s and 1980s), the FCC required telephone companies to sell equipment through separate subsidiaries, thus "facilitating competition in the equipment market" that led to an "explosive growth in the variety of end user devices."[91] As former FCC Chairman Reed Hundt noted:

> "Today, the benefits of competition in the CPE market are tangible. Consumers can buy telephones of all shapes, sizes and colors with a bewildering array of features and functions. They can buy telephones with built-in answering machines, telephones with memory, telephones with speed dialing, and cordless telephones."

> "Since deregulation, prices for this equipment have fallen, and as prices declined, sales increased. Sales of cordless telephones, for example, increased from approximately 4 million units in 1985 to 9 million units in 1992."[92]

The *Carterfone* decision resulted in huge benefits to consumers who were offered a multiplicity of new telephone equipment and functions (see box), but the decision is even more lauded today for its role in enabling the growth of the Internet. As a former FCC colleague wrote:

> "Most important for the growth and development of the Internet, the Commission's deregulation of customer premises equipment, or CPE, cleared the way for the rapid deployment of the modem. … In fact, without Part 68, users of the public switched network would not have been able to connect their computers and modems to the network, and it is likely that the Internet would have been unable to develop."[93]

In addition, though it is not widely acknowledged, *Carterfone* was critical not only to the development of the Internet but also to the data communications industry (consisting of companies like IBM and DEC) that preceded it.[94]

Regulation 517, 520-32 (1988) *excerpted in* Thomas Krattenmaker, *Telecommunications Law and Policy* (1998) at 361.

[90] *See* Jonathan E. Nuechterlein and Philip J. Weiser, *Digital Crossroads: American Telecommunications Policy in the Internet Age* (2005) at 58-59.

[91] Nuechterlein and Weiser, *Digital Crossroads* at 59.

[92] Reed E. Hundt, *Statement,* Committee on Commerce, Science, and Transp., U.S Senate, February 23, 1994.

---

[93] Jason Oxman, *The FCC and the Unregulation of the Internet* (OPP Working Paper, July 1999) at 14.

[94] For example, at the time of the Carterfone decision, technology experts were developing "sophisticated data communications networks using combinations of dialup modems with acoustical couplers (rather than the direct connections that Carterfone allowed) and private lines with directly connected modems—all connecting to, for example, the early time-sharing computers," to create what was known as Remote Access Data Processing. In addition, public packet switching was also developed in the form of X.25 networks that preceded the development of the Internet. *Email communication with Dale Hatfield, March 21, 2010.*

Direct-Broadcast Satellite (DBS) (1982)

Stakeholders

The FCC received the first application for a license to offer satellite television from the Satellite Television Corporation in 1980, shortly after the ITU designated the 12.2-12.7 GHz band for Broadcast Satellite Services. Several other applications soon followed, from CBS, Direct Broadcast Satellite Corporation, RCA, United States Satellite Broadcasting Corporation and Western Union.[95]

Broadcasters (e.g., NBC, the Association of Maximum Service Television) and several public interest groups (e.g., the United Church of Christ), and others (e.g., the American Newspaper Publishers Association, the American Petroleum Institute, the Association of American Railroads) opposed the applications.

What did the FCC do?

The FCC authorized DBS service, amended the Table of Frequency Allocations to permit DBS downlink operations in the 12.2-12.7 GHz band and uplink operations in the 17.3-17.8 GHz band, and adopted rules to prevent harmful interference to DBS operators from terrestrial licensees in the 12 GHz band.[96]

The FCC also decided to adopt a "flexible regulatory approach" to DBS systems, permitting DBS providers to choose to operate either as broadcasters or common carriers or both (i.e., as a broadcaster on some channels and a common carrier on others) and declined to impose ownership restrictions or access requirements.[97]

Options

i. Deny the application on the grounds that the benefits to the public do not justify using the spectrum and orbital slots for DBS;

ii. Permit use of the orbital slots and spectrum to provide broadcast video to unserved rural areas;

iii. Allocate only a portion of the 500 MHz for DBS while retaining the balance for private microwave uses;

iv. Allocate the entire 500 MHz for DBS and grant the applications because DBS potentially had a unique capability to provide service to rural and other unserved areas; would increase competition and diversity by offering additional programming to the public; could introduce new video services such as high-definition TV; and would promote the satellite communications industry.

v. Impose a traditional broadcast regulatory framework for DBS or adopt minimal regulation.

---

[95] Inquiry into the Development of Regulatory Policy in Regard to Direct Broadcast Satellites, 90 FCC 2d 676 (1982) at ¶¶ 2-5.

[96] Direct Broadcast Satellites, 90 FCC 2d 676, at ¶¶ 7, 59-77.
[97] Direct Broadcast Satellites, 90 FCC 2d 676, at ¶¶ 78-101.

The FCC's rationale for its actions

The FCC concluded that DBS would give high-quality television service to as many as 11 million people in rural areas who in 1981 had no on-air reception or got fewer than 3 channels and who would be willing to pay as much as 5 percent of their income for this service.[98]

The FCC also determined that viewers in urban areas would highly value the additional options for television viewing that DBS could provide.[99]

Overall, the FCC concluded that the benefits of DBS far outweighed any adverse impact DBS would have on local broadcasting, and would also constitute efficient spectrum utilization.[100]

DBS' Shaky Start

None of the applicants survived (at least until one or two resurfaced in the 1990s), sunk by the high cost of launching satellites (estimated at $700 million in the first year) and the lack of programming that differentiated DBS from on-air television.

Edward A. Comor, *Communication, Commerce, and Power: The Political Economy of America and the Direct Broadcast Satellite, 1960-2000* (1998) at 60-63.

Program Access: Key to the Growth of DBS

Congress went further than the FCC and enacted the "program access" requirements (section 628), which essentially enabled DBS to get the right to offer cable content to its viewers on non-discriminatory terms.

See Daniel Brenner *et al, Cable Television and Other Nonbroadcast Video: Law and Policy,* at 15-9.

Impact of the decision: the long view

Although the FCC "moved with the regulatory speed of light" in approving this new service, the market was slow to follow.[101] (See box, left)

DBS, thus, at least initially was seen as a major flop: "the 1983-84 disaster of DBS was on such a scale as to somewhat depress the entire business of space satellites."[102]

Cable companies, fearing the threat from DBS, denied emerging DBS operators like DirecTV access to programming, and also formed their own DBS operator (Primestar), which led to an antitrust lawsuit filed by the New York Attorney General.[103]

Congress then stepped in and helped DBS by enacting the Satellite Home Viewer Act in 1988 which allows satellite carriers to deliver broadcast programming to satellite viewers who were unable to receive broadcast programming ("unserved

---

[98] Direct Broadcast Satellites, 90 FCC 2d 676, at ¶¶13-14.
[99] Direct Broadcast Satellites, 90 FCC 2d 676, at ¶¶15-20.
[100] Direct Broadcast Satellites, 90 FCC 2d 676, at ¶ 21. *See* Staff Report, *Policies for Regulation of Direct Broadcast Satellites* (Office of Plans and Policy, September 1980) at 87 ("most forms of regulation now imposed by the Commission will prove unnecessary or counterproductive.").

[101] Sterling and Kittross, *Stay Tuned,* at 573.
[102] Comor, *Communication, Commerce, and Power*, at 63.
[103] Comor, *Communication, Commerce, and Power*, at 166-168.

households"). [104] In 1992, Congress went further and enacted the "program access" requirements (section 628), which essentially enabled DBS to get the right to offer cable content to its viewers on non-discriminatory terms. [105]

An ongoing issue for regulators is whether (or when) these "program access" rules should be ended. If the rules are continued too long, there is a danger of harm to the competitive process. As Shapiro and Varian have stated:

> "Regulations like these, which control and circumscribe the vertical relationships between those who produce content and distribute it, are increasingly out of place as the creation of content and distribution of information become more and more competitive....
>
> Hopefully, the monopoly power enjoyed by cable operators will also erode as broadcast satellite becomes a stronger force and as telephone companies enter into multichannel video distribution. In this setting, regulations on vertical relationships in the information sector may well serve to benefit certain special interests rather then the public interest." [106]

In 1994, DirecTV became the first DBS system in operation in the United States and quickly became a popular service, signing up close to 10 million subscribers by 2000. [107]

In 2006, a Kagan report showed that cable's market share had dropped more than 20 points throughout the previous 10 years as DBS added about 25 million subscribers. In 10 years, Kagan projects net new DBS subscribers will grow more than 6 million to more than 33.5 million by 2015. [108]

---

[104] Comor, *Communication, Commerce, and Power,* at 168; Stuart Minor Benjamin, Douglas Gary Lichtman, Howard A. Shelanski, *Telecommunications Law and Policy (*2001) at 549 (Congress created a compulsory license which permits satellite carriers to deliver network programming to unserved viewers without the copyright owners permission).

[105] Stuart Minor Benjamin et al., *Telecommunications Law and Policy,* at 500. Congress stepped in again in 1999 with further revisions that imposed additional requirements on DBS but also permitted them to carry local signals. Stuart Minor Benjamin et al., *Telecommunications Law and Policy,* at 550-557.

[106] *See* Shapiro and Varian, *Information Rules,* at 312. The Commission extended the program access rules for an additional five years, beginning in 2007. Review of the Commission's

Program Access Rules and Examination of Programming Tying Arrangements*, Report and Order,* 22 FCC Rcd 17791 (rel. October 1, 2007).

[107] Sterling and Kittross, *Stay Tuned,* at 597. DBS service started in 1989 in the United Kingdom (as BSkyB), and had grown to serve 5.5 million households by 1996; in Europe the Astra system was serving over 65 million homes by the end of 1995. Comor, *Communication, Commerce, and Power,* at 166.

[108] *See "DBS subscribers to reach 33.5 million by 2015, says Kagan Research",* available at http://broadcastengineering.com/news/dbs_subscribers_33million_2015/.

Digital Cell Phones (1988-94)

"In comparison to its policy of the early 1980s in the AMPS cellular bands, the FCC did not mandate a specific standard for the PCS bands. Carriers were free to choose whatever standard they wished."[109]

Stakeholders

In 1988, American cellular firms disagreed about whether the FCC or the market should set the digital cellular standard. Northern Telecom, for instance, argued that market forces should determine the "precise digital radio standard (e.g., channel coding) and basic technologies (e.g., Frequency Division Multiple Access or Time Division Multiple Access) to be used." PacTel Cellular and Bell Atlantic Mobile Systems urged the FCC to begin a rulemaking to set the digital standards.[110] The Telecommunications Industry Association began work on developing a voluntary standard for next generation cellular systems.

In the early 1990s, Qualcomm entered the picture, proposing a new standard, based on Code Division Multiple Access (CDMA), which offered significant new capabilities:

> "Whereas D-AMPS would roughly double the number of calls possible per chunk of spectrum, CDMA promised between ten and twenty times as many calls compared to the old AMPS [standard] …; the battery life of terminals would be longer and fewer (expensive) terminals would be needed."[111]

Options

i. Let the market decide what standard to use to provide advanced cellular services;

ii. Codify a consensus standard developed by industry;

iii. Mandate a standard in a rulemaking.

What did the FCC do?

Although the FCC had set the AMPS standard for analog cellular in 1979, by the mid-1980s the FCC favored a more flexible approach.[112]

Thus, the FCC declined in 1988 to adopt a single standard; instead letting market forces determine which standard to adopt.[113]

In its 1988 decision, the FCC stated:

> "We believe it would be premature for the Commission to intervene in the standard setting process. Industry is in a better position to evaluate the technical advantages and disadvantages of the various advanced cellular technologies and develop approaches to compatibility."[114]

The FCC also did not want to engage in the delays that may have occurred in a rulemaking, and believed that industry was best suited for developing a standard.[115]

---

[109] N.Gandal *et al*, Standards in Wireless Networks, *Telecommunications Policy* 27 (2003) at 327.

[110] Amendment of Parts 2 and 22 of the Commission's rules to Permit Liberalization of Technology and Auxiliary Service Offerings in eh Domestic Public Cellular Radio Telecommunications Service, 3 FCC Rcd 7033 (1988) at 7040.

[111] Jacques Pelkmans, "The GSM Standard: Explaining a European Success Story, *Journal of European Public Policy* (2001) at 448.

[112] *See* N.Gandal *et al*, Standards in Wireless Networks, *Telecommunications Policy* at 327.

[113] Amendment of Parts 2 and 22 of the Commission's rules, 3 FCC Rcd at 7040.

[114] Amendment of Parts 2 and 22 of the Commission's rules, 3 FCC Rcd at ¶ 51.

[115] Amendment of Parts 2 and 22 of the Commission's rules, 3 FCC Rcd at 7040.

In 1992, in the PCS docket, the FCC affirmed that it would not set a single standard, stating that:

> "Although we do not propose to require specific standards at this time, commenters are free to suggest areas in which specific standards may be beneficial and ways to expedite this process should it become necessary in the future."[116]

Impact of the decision: the long view

* The US and Europe took very different paths: a market-oriented approach in the US and a centrally mandated solution in Europe.[117] *Business Week* described this as, "The Cowboys vs. the Committee."[118]

* In the U.S., there are three incompatible systems vying for leadership: GSM, TDMA (a "close cousin" of GSM) and CDMA.[119] They are incompatible in this sense:

> "Consumers buying a phone for one system will not be able to switch to another without buying an expensive new phone. However, they are compatible in the sense that users of one system can make calls to users on another system."[120]

* There is a widespread perception that the European decision was a tremendous success:

> "In retrospect, no one can doubt that [the European] decision was inspired. After all, it has become a main

European strength, so that nowadays GSM is the most extended standard in the world (with the main exception of the United States)."[121]

* *Business Week* noted in 1998 that:

> "For the US, the costs of playing second fiddle are now painfully obvious. Dataquest, Inc. figures that cellular subscribers worldwide spent upwards of $37 billion on handsets last year. That number will shoot past $55 billion in 2001. Washington-based market researcher Strategis Group says most of that growth will be in phones built to Europe's GSM specs—further enriching Nokia and Ericsson. Of the 98.6 million digital cell phones produced last year, 58% were GSM, according to Dataquest."[122]

* Even in North America, American equipment suppliers took a beating:

---

[116] Amendment of the Commission's Rules to Establish New Personal Communications Services, 7 FCC Rcd 5676 (1992) at ¶108, n.79.
[117] Shapiro and Varian, *Information Rules,* at 264.
[118] "Cell Phones: Europe Made the Right Call," *Business Week,* 9/7/98 at 107-110.
[119] Shapiro and Varian, *Information Rules,* at 265. *See* David Horne, *Market Oriented Spectrum Policy Evolution in the United States,* Intel Corp. (2009) at 18.
[120] Shapiro and Varian, *Information Rules,* at 265.

[121] Lucio Fuentelsaz *et al*, "The Evolution of mobile communications in Europe: The Transition from the second to the third generation," *Telecommunications Policy* 32 (2008) at 437. *See* N.Gandal *et al*, Standards in Wireless Networks, *Telecommunications Policy,* at 326 (many have argued that Europe's decision was a great success and the US decision was a great failure); Jacques Pelkmans, "The GSM Standard: Explaining a European Success Story, *Journal of European Public Policy* at 449 ("Far from being a disaster, the US approach could, nonetheless, be regarded as mistaken."). *See also* Shapiro and Varian, *Information Rules,* at 263-264 (Europe adopted new digital wireless technology more rapidly than in the US.); T.R. Reid, *The United States of Europe: the New Superpower and the End of American Supremacy* 92004) at 126 ("the Europeans, with their GSM technology, had sprinted ahead of the American leader."); Walter Mossberg, "Free my Phone, *Wall Street Journal,* http://mossblog.allthingsd.com/20071021/free-my-phone ("Because the federal government failed to set a standard for wireless technology years ago, we have two major, incompatible technologies in the U.S.").
[122] *Business Week,* 9/7/98 at 107-110.

Motorola's share of the US market fell from 60% in 1994 to 34% in 1998.[123]

* GSM's global dominance is further suggested by the fact that 675 operators in 210 countries have adopted the GSM standard.[124]

* However, the picture is not as bleak from the American perspective. When comparing economies of scale (which is one of the presumed benefits of a uniform standard), the European advantage diminishes over time: the semiconductor costs of TDMA and GSM handsets have fallen in unison. Thus, one analyst argues that: "This indicates that the actual benefits of economies of scale reach the point of diminishing return well below the level implied as an advantage via the single market homogeneity approach."[125] In other words, US manufacturers may be able to achieve the same economies of scale even if their sales volumes (60 million subscribers for TDMA) are well below the GSM volume (273 million subscribers).[126]

* By other indicators as well, the data show that American consumers pay less on a per minute basis and use their cell phones for longer than either Europeans or Japanese:

	Minutes of use/	Revenue per minute
U.S.	812	$0.06
W. Europe	161	$0.20
Japan	138	$0.26

Based on these numbers, the FCC concluded in January, 2009, that "U.S. mobile subscribers continue to fare extremely well relative to mobile subscribers in Western Europe and comparable Asia-Pacific

countries."[127] The FCC also noted that mobile penetration in Europe was very high "due in part to greater use of prepaid service plans and ownership of multiple devices or subscriber identity module ("SIM") cards."[128] The SIM option was included in the GSM standard adopted by European regulators but is not freely available to most U.S. consumers.

* CDMA may also have technical advantages over GSM, such as increased efficiency (meaning that the carrier can serve more subscribers), lower power requirements, and the need for fewer cell towers (because less cell-to-cell coordination is needed by operators).[129]

* The European advantage, if any, did not last even through the transition from the second to the third generation of wireless services.[130]

---

[127] Annual Report and Analysis of Competitive Market Conditions with Respect to Commercial Mobile Services, *Thirteenth Report,* -- FCC Rcd ---- (2009), http://hraunfoss.fcc.gov/edocs_public/attachmatch/DA-09-54A1.pdf , at ¶¶ 218-220.
[128] *Thirteenth Report, supra.* at ¶ 221. A SIM card or *Subscriber Identity Module* is a portable memory chip used in some models of cellular telephones. The SIM card makes it easy to switch to a new phone by simply sliding the SIM out of the old phone and into the new one. The SIM holds personal identity information, cell phone number, phone book, text messages and other data. http://www.wisegeek.com/what-is-a-sim-card.htm
[129] Ed Sutherland, "GSM vs. CDMA," http://www.m-indya.com/gsm/CDMA-vs-GSM.htm. *See generally* Marc Delprat and Vinod Kumar, "Second Generation Systems," in Jerry D. Gibson, editor, *The Mobile Communications Handbook* (1996).
[130] *See* Lucio Fuentelsaz *et al,* "The Evolution of mobile communications in Europe: The Transition from the second to the third generation," *Telecommunications Policy* at 447 (global success of GSM led to prediction of similar success for UMTS, which has not materialized).

---

[123] *Business Week,* 9/7/98 at 107-110.
[124] Lucio Fuentelsaz *et al,* The Evolution of mobile communications in Europe, *Telecommunications Policy* at 439.
[125] David Horne, *Market Oriented Spectrum Policy Evolution in the United States* at 22.
[126] David Horne, *Market Oriented Spectrum Policy Evolution in the United States* at 22.

High Definition and Digital Television (1987-1997)

At the outset, it is worth noting the differences between high-definition television and digital television. HDTV refers to a level of picture quality. Digital television (DTV) refers to a type of transmission. HDTV can be analog or digital and DTV can be high-definition or standard definition. Broadcasters can send HDTV or DTV signals, and so can cable and satellite operators.[131]

In terms of policy, too, there are several issues at play. "Repacking" is the freeing up spectrum from one use and designating it for a different use, e.g., broadcast to wireless services. "Multicasting" enables broadcasters to choose to use the available spectrum to offer multiple viewing channels rather than a single HD channel.

Over a period of several years, the FCC became the battleground for a major, high-stakes showdown involving spectrum, technical standards, and global trade.

Stakeholders

In the late 1980s, land mobile operators had almost persuaded the FCC to reallocate unused broadcast spectrum for law enforcement and other purposes, but broadcasters fought to preserve their stake in the spectrum by arguing the spectrum was needed to provide HDTV.[132]

FCC Chairman Dennis Patrick created the Advisory Committee on Advanced Television Standards in 1988 and appointed former FCC Chairman Richard Wiley as its Chairman.[133] Wiley challenged innovators to develop the best technical standards and equipment and to submit them for testing by the FCC's Advisory Panel, which would declare a winner.

The standards battle pitted four main teams of engineers and innovators: (1) NHK, the Japanese public broadcasting company; (2) Zenith and AT&T; (3) General Instrument and MIT; and (4) Philips, Sarnoff Research Labs, NBC and Thomson, working together as the Advanced Television Research Consortium. In May 1993, NHK, which had proposed the only non-digital HDTV system, dropped out, and the remaining 3 teams formed a *"Grand Alliance"* in which they agreed to merge their technologies and engage in cross-licensing.[134]

Computer companies and movie studios, also joined the standards battle, insisting that any HDTV standard should include a progressive scanning industry specification (rather than interlacing), in order to facilitate convergence between the television and personal computer industries.[135]

The NAB opposed any requirement that broadcasters must use the second channel for HDTV, but the Big 3 networks and some programmers supported requiring a minimum amount of HDTV programming.[136]

Options

Allocations:

i. Allocate unused broadcast spectrum for Land Mobile; or

---

[131] Stuart Minor Benjamin et al., *Telecommunications Law and Policy,* at 332.
[132] Joel Brinkley, *Defining Vision: The Battle for the Future of Television* (1997) at 25-27.
[133] Brinkley, *Defining Vision,* at 30-31.

[134] Shapiro and Varian, *Information Rules,* at 221; Brinkley, *Defining Vision,* at 225-244, 247-263.
[135] Shapiro and Varian, *Information Rules,* at 221; Brinkley, *Defining Vision,* at 278.
[136] Advanced Telecommunications Services, *Fifth Report and Order*, April 3, 1997 at ¶¶ 38-39.

ii. Permit broadcasters to use the second channel to provide HDTV (or any digital services).

Standards:

i. Accept the existing Japanese analog standard for HDTV on 8 MHz channels as the world standard [as suggested initially by the industry standards body, ATSC, and the State Department];
ii. Follow the European example by spending hundreds of millions of dollars of government funding to develop the best technological solution [as some in Congress were advocating, though without support from the Administration];
iii. Let industry develop a standard, working through an Advisory Committee appointed by the FCC.

Mandate HDTV?
i. Require all broadcasters to offer HDTV programming on the second channel.
ii. Permit broadcasters to decide whether and how much HDTV to offer, while requiring they offer digital TV.

What did the FCC do?

Allocating spectrum: The FCC backed off from proposals to allocate unused broadcast spectrum for Land Mobile, after being persuaded by broadcasters they needed the spectrum for HDTV.[137]

HDTV standards: From 1988-1992, the FCC generally supported the efforts of the

Advisory Committee to challenge the private sector to develop an HDTV standard. The FCC also adopted a series of key orders:

* In 1988, the FCC set forth the general principles for guiding its decisions on advanced television, including that spectrum would be allocated from the spectrum currently allocated for broadcast; analog service must continue during the transition.[138]

* In 1990, the FCC decided to require "simulcasting" of the analog and advanced services on 6 MHZ channels.[139]

* In 1991, the FCC proposed that only current broadcast licensees would be eligible to receive licenses for the new service, and that the NTSC license should be surrendered after the conversion.[140] In 1996, Congress instructed the Commission to restrict eligibility to those who held a broadcast license (or those who had filed applications for construction permits) as of October 24, 1991.[141]

* In 1996, the FCC approved the "Grand Alliance" standards that combined the best technical innovations of its members.[142] Specifically, the FCC adopted the ATSC DTV standard, except with respect to the video format layer, which remained optional.[143] The FCC noted that the DTV

---

[137] In re Further Sharing of the UHF Television Band by Private Land Mobile Radio Operators, *Notice of Proposed Rulemaking*, 101 F.C.C. 2d 852 (1985) (proposing to move spectrum for land mobile use in New York City, Los Angeles, Chicago, Philadelphia, San Francisco, Washington D.C., Houston and Dallas); In re Further Sharing of the UHF Television Band by Private Land Mobile Radio Operators, *Order*, 2 FCC Rcd 6441 (1987) (deferring action on sharing UHF spectrum between TV stations and private land mobile until HDTV issues are resolved). *See* Brinkley, *Defining Vision*, at 27.

[138] Advanced Telecommunications Systems, *Second Inquiry*, 3 FCC Rcd 6520, 6525, 6530 (1988).
[139] Advanced Telecommunications Systems, *First Order*, 5 FCC Rcd 5627, 5627-5629 (1990).
[140] Advanced Telecommunications Systems, *Notice of Proposed Rulemaking*, 6 FCC Rcd 7024 (1991).
[141] 47 U.S.C. Sec. 336 (a)(1).
[142] Advanced Telecommunications Systems, *Fourth R&O*, 11 FCC Rcd 17771 (1996) at ¶ 31. Shapiro and Varian, *Information Rules*, at 220-221; Brinkley, *Defining Vision*, at 247-263.
[143] Sterling and Kittross, *Stay Tuned*, at 604, give details of the ATSC standard:

standard "is flexible and extensible and permits data broadcasting as well as new services."[144]

* In 1997, the FCC declined to require broadcasters to use the second channel for HDTV but instead let broadcasters decide to offer HDTV based on their own assessment of consumer demand.[145]

Keeping Spectrum for Broadcast Use

"[B]y scaring Congress with the prospect of the Japanese beating out the United States in HDTV, broadcasters were able to preserve for themselves vacant channel space in the UHF portion of the spectrum that was in danger of being reassigned to uses other than television. Remember this key point as the HDTV story unfolds: the broadcasters have long lusted after more free spectrum space but never had much appetite for HDTV itself."

Shapiro and Varian, *Information Rules,* at 220

"The FCC's 1996 decision, which was quite detailed with respect to channel allotment, audio, and such details as aspect ratio (adopting a widescreen ratio of 16:9 rather than the familiar 4:3) allowed up to 18 different video formats, some providing 1080 lines of vertical definition (as contrasted to the 525-line NTSC standard adopted in 1941), but some supplying only 480 lines—which since they are digital, still provided a sharper picture than analog sets. To complicate things further, some broadcasters planned to use interlaced scanning (i), and others the progressive (p) scanning used for most computer monitors."

[144] Advanced Telecommunications Systems, *Fourth R&O,* 11 FCC Rcd at 17789.
[145] Advanced Telecommunications Systems, *Fifth R&O,* 12 FCC Rcd 12809 (1997) at 12826-12827.

The FCC's rationale for its actions

Allocations: The FCC backed away from requiring broadcasters to share the spectrum with land mobile operators after concluding that broadcasters may need the spectrum for HDTV, which was emerging as a trade war issue for the US against perceived Japanese dominance.[146] There was strong congressional support for HDTV and the broadcasters' position.[147]

Standards: Twice previously, in 1950 with respect to color TV and in 1982 with respect to AM stereo, FCC attempts to mandate technical standards had resulted in failure.[148] Those experiences may have led the FCC, at least initially, to step aside and let industry develop the HDTV standard. After the Advisory Committee proposed the "Grand Alliance" standard to the FCC, there was an additional debate about whether the Commission should mandate the standard or permit industry to choose. Broadcasters, equipment manufacturers, and consumer groups argued that the Commission should mandate standards because "startup, coordination and splintering problems are more severe than those of other industries."[149] Cable operators and computer

---

[146] Further Sharing of the UHF Television Band by Private Land Mobile Radio Services, *Order*, 2 FCC Rcd 6441(1987) (Deferring action on a proposal to reallocate unassigned UHF television channels to the private mobile services pending resolution of an ongoing proceeding before the advisory committee on advanced television systems).
[147] Brinkley, *Defining Vision,* at 37-42.
[148] See e.g., Joseph Farrell and Carl Shapiro, *"Standard Setting in High Definition Television,"* Brookings Papers (1992) at 21("FCC appears to be painfully aware of the AM stereo debacle ..."), 52 ("Despite the FCC's endorsement of the CBS system, there was virtually no development of the color television industry using it.").
[149] Advanced Telecommunications Systems, *Fourth R&O,* 11 FCC Rcd at 17777. "Startup" refers to the situation where everyone would be better off adopting a new technology but no one has the incentive to move first. "Coordination"

companies argued that all the parties had a strong incentive to reach a consensus on a standard without a governmental mandate. The FCC decided to mandate a standard to provide "reliability" and "certainty" as broadcasting entered the digital era.[150]

Impact of the decision: the long view

* When the FCC took up the repacking issue in 1987, it faced a zero-sum choice: broadcasters or wireless services. In the early 1990s, as part of the FCC-sponsored competition to develop HDTV, General Instruments proposed an all-digital system that later became adopted by all the participants.

With digital, the FCC no longer had to make a zero-sum choice. Spectrum was available for broadcast as well as other wireless uses. Thus, in 1992, the Commission allocated 220 MHz for "broadband PCS" in the 1.85-2.20 GHz band.[151]

* The FCC also made additional spectrum available for wireless services by allowing broadcasters to choose between HDTV and multicasting, rather than mandating that broadcasters offer HDTV. Thus, in 1997, the FCC reallocated 108 MHZ of the 402 MHz that had been allocated for terrestrial television broadcasting, leaving 294 MHz for TV.

Of the 108 MHz, 24 MHz was allocated for public safety, 6 MHz for guard bands, and the balance for flexible use—30 MHz in the upper 700 MHz band (746-806 MHz, channels 60-69) and 48 MHz in the lower 700 MHz band (698-746 MHz, channels 52-

59).[152] These spectrum bands may not have been available if the FCC had required broadcasters to transmit only HDTV programming.[153]

* The FCC's decision to not require HDTV carriage satisfied economists who were puzzled that broadcasters would use valuable spectrum for a service for which there was, at that time, little consumer demand, given the high cost of HDTV sets and the paucity of HDTV programming.[154]

* Overall, these developments, along with a series of later decisions by the FCC, helped speed up the transition to digital TV but may not have done much for promoting sales of HDTV sets, at least for another decade.[155]

* In terms of global trade, the gains for the U.S. may not have materialized, as described below:

> "The real winner of the Grand Alliance technology is not the United States or U.S. companies—which will only collect royalty fees, but Thomson of France and Philips of the Netherlands—which will manufacture the product for consumer use."[156]

---

refs to collaborative efforts by the parties. "Splintering" refers to the breakdown of consensus. *Id.*

[150] Advanced Telecommunications Systems, *Fourth R&O,* 11 FCC Rcd at 17787-17791.

[151] Redevelopment of Spectrum to Encourage Innovation in the Use of New Telecommunications Technologies, *First Report and Order,* 7 FCC Rcd 6886 (1992).

[152] Evan Kwerel, and Jonathan Levy, "The DTV Transition in the U.S.," in Martin Cave and Kyoshi Nakamura, Editors, *Digital Broadcasting: Policy and Practice in the Americas, Europe and Japan* (2006) at 25.

[153] *See* Reed Hundt, *You Say You Want a Revolution: A Story of Information Age Politics* (2000) at 63-64, 210.

[154] *See e.g.,* Farrell and Shapiro, *"Standard Setting in High Definition Television"* at 80-81 (comments of Roger Noll).

[155] Shapiro and Varian, *Information Rules,* at 223.

[156] Michael Dupagne and Peter B. Seel, *HDTV: A Global Perspective,* at 165.

Lessons Learned

> "As so often had been the case in communications, the path of development was not easily diverted from familiar channels….<u>Change would come, but it would come slowly</u>. Even today much of the system of power established by the early decisions remains with us—and the media those decisions helped to create is now ubiquitous and inescapable."

Starr, *The Creation of the Media,* at 384 (emphasis added).

The following is a summary of the main lessons learned from a review of the FCC decisions discussed in the previous sections:

Radio: The charm of early radio was that "experimentation, spontaneity and content aimed at small audiences were common."[157] The FRC disfavored this type of content as narrowly-focused propaganda, and instead adopted rules that resulted in the growth of commercial radio financed by advertising revenues. Although commercial radio produced a Golden Age of programming in the late 1930s,[158] the question remains whether the FRC's decision to favor corporate-sponsored networks—rather than the multiplicity of diverse non-commercial stations-- best served the public interest. The FRC performed a valuable service by helping to create commercial networks but did so at the cost of achieving diversity. Yet, today, there is a strong push to see just such diversity in broadcast programming on radio and television.[159]

Also, as we will see, the focus on developing national networks for radio contrasts with the focus on achieving localism for broadcast television. Here, too, there are mixed results. As Starr notes, while the FRC did succeed in creating national radio networks, there was an implicit tradeoff: "more equal access to listening meant more concentrated control of broadcasting."[160]

Broadcast Television: Unlike the decisions concerning radio, the FCC's decisions on broadcast television did not as easily achieve the desired results. For example, although FM radio gained more channels in the 1945 allocations, the number of stations shrank and the creator of FM radio, Edwin Armstrong, lost, as the FCC decision rendered obsolete 400,000-500,000 radio sets. FM radio did not start to grow again until the 1960s.

Additionally, though the FCC approved CBS' color standard in 1950, the company did not make many sets because the sets were unable to receive black and white transmissions which consumers continued to want. As late as 1963, only 3% of households had color sets. Yet, it is not just the decisions concerning FM radio or color TV but the entire package of decisions concerning broadcast television that is justly criticized. Overall, the result for most Americans was less choice: fewer on-air stations and confusion resulting from the failures of the FCC's intermixture policy.

With the benefit of hindsight, it appears that a better outcome could have been achieved by delaying the 1945 allocation decision until enough information was available to set the color standard (as CBS had urged), and later assigning channels in the UHF

---

[157] Berresford, *"How Government Can Bring New Communications to All Americans,"* at 14 (noting that early radio content was "talk, ethnic nationality hours, labor news, church news, and vaudeville-type musical entertainment by hometown, often ethnic talent").

[158] Sterling and Kittross, *Stay Tuned,* at 181-200.

[159] *See e.g.,* Eric Klinenberg, *Fighting for Air: The Battle to Control America's Media* (2007), esp. ch.8 ('Fighting for Air'), ch. 9 ("The Media

---

and Democracy") and ch. 10 ("Low Power to the People").

[160] Starr, *The Creation of the Media,* at 350.

band for TV.[161] A better alternative for FM may have been for the FCC to adopt the compromise 50-68 MHz allocation (rather than moving FM to 88-108 MHz), which the industry believed "will not cripple FM."[162] This would have enabled FM radio to continue its growth without a decades-long interruption, produced better quality color TV (including in higher definition), and avoided the engineering hassles and delay that lasted through the 1950s to determine whether communities should receive TV broadcasts from VHF or UHF stations or some mixture of the two.

In addition, the Commission may have missed an opportunity to create 6-7 national TV channels, rather than the 3-4 that finally emerged. An increase in the number of channels would likely have meant more program diversity.[163] As noted with regard to radio, national licenses may also have resulted in greater ownership concentration. These tradeoffs present complex policy choices that warrant further study.

Cable Television: In the early 1960s, cable TV showed promise as an alternative distribution mechanism to broadcast TV. In the preceding decade, new cable systems were introduced at an annual rate of 24.9 percent and subscriber growth was about 40 percent annually. More than 1 million homes out of 60 million received cable, and more than 1,200 systems were operating. However, this rapid growth dropped dramatically as a result of the Commission's 1966 regulation of the cable industry.

Beginning in 1966, off-air broadcasters gained protection from a Commission hostile to cable operators. Had the Commission continued with its policies, especially hostility to pay TV, cable TV would have been put out of business or left to serve only remote locations unable to receive broadcast signals. Instead, as "evidence accumulated that the FCC rationale for regulating cable was flawed,"[164] the Commission shifted course. For the next two decades, cable was progressively deregulated, with a key boost from the FCC's Open Skies policies that facilitated cheaper distribution of video programming and the *Home Box Office* decision that paved the way for pay TV on cable.[165]

A postscript is worth noting: as cable TV grew and prospered and demonstrated market power from its monopoly position in some communities, Congress, the FCC, and local jurisdictions responded by imposing rate regulation and other restrictions.[166]

Carterfone: The Commission long resisted innovators' efforts to attach devices to AT&T's phone lines. If not for *Carterfone*, rotary-dial telephone handsets (in black) may have been the only available option for consumers, instead of the multiplicity of choice consumers now have. However, although *Carterfone* opened the door in 1968, consumers did not benefit from

---

[161] *See e.g.,* Slotten, *Radio and Television Regulation,* at 229 ("Without falling into the fallacy of counterfactual history, we can conclude that CBS' system might have been successful had it received more support from industry and the FCC. It probably stood the best chance of success in 1947, before monochrome television became completely entrenched.").

[162] Slotten, *Radio and Television Regulation,* at 132 (quoting the President of Zenith Radio). This presumes that the concerns about interference could have been resolved. *Supra*, p.8, n.36.

[163] Noll *et al, Economic Aspects of Television Regulation,* at 101. ("[A]n increase in the number of channels … would enable minority tastes to be met with less loss of conventional fare.").

[164] Besen *et al,*" The Deregulation of Cable Television," 44 *Law and Contemporary Problems,* at 122.

[165] Sterling and Kittross, *Stay Tuned,* at 468. *See generally,* Daniel Brenner *et al, Cable Television and Other Nonbroadcast Video: Law and Policy* (2004) at 2-10 to 2-22 (discussing the 1992 Cable Act and its precedents).

[166] Sterling and Kittross, *Stay Tuned,* at 417-418; Crawford, "Cable Regulation in the Satellite Era," at 6-11.

having a choice of telephone handsets for many years, because it took the FCC another

7 years to develop the Part 68 rules and even longer for the "separate subsidiaries" requirement that led to the growth of a competitive market for telephone handsets and other equipment.

In addition, without *Carterfone,* the result may have been an Internet that would have taken much longer to develop because telephone users were prohibited from attaching devices to their telephone. Instead, the decision led to rules permitting modems for Internet access over phone lines—in addition to its significant pre-Internet contribution towards creating a robust and competitive data communications market.

Direct-Broadcast Satellite (DBS): The DBS story offers a clear example of effective governmental action to encourage entry into monopoly markets by awarding government franchises to new entrants.[167] However, as demonstrated by the initial failure of DBS operators in the years immediately following the franchise awards, additional help was needed: access to the programming carried by cable operators. DBS, though authorized in 1982, reemerged as a commercial service only in 1994, six years after Congress passed program access legislation.

With the benefit of ongoing regulatory and legislative support, the result is a service that now has 25-30 million subscribers and has emerged as a strong competitor in the market for video services.

Digital cell phones: The FCC did not adopt any transmission standards but let carriers decide which standard to adopt. In the U.S. that resulted in three different standards: TDMA, GSM, and CDMA. The "market" approach was faulted by those who argued the U.S. lost ground to Europe, which mandated GSM as the standard for digital cellular. Yet, for both consumers and U.S. firms, the FCC's decision to give carriers the

---

[167] *See* Shapiro and Varian, *Information Rules,* at 313.

27

flexibility to develop their own standards may turn out to be a good decision in the long run.

Overall, American consumers are benefiting from lower prices and greater usage, so it may mean little whether the U.S. should have mandated a standard or let the market set it. European consumers, however, have an advantage in being able to use SIM cards to switch carriers to obtain the best service. The SIM option was included in the GSM standard adopted by European regulators but is not freely available to most U.S. consumers.

From a trade perspective, because this is not a winner-take-all market, U.S. companies, as well as those from Europe, have been able to achieve significant gains.

High Definition (HDTV) and Digital Television (DTV):

The race to develop HDTV produced a major technological breakthrough (i.e., digitization of HDTV) and consumer gains such as a better quality television picture. Overall, these developments, along with a series of later decisions by the FCC, helped speed up the transition to digital TV.

With the fundamental shift to an all-digital system, the FCC was also able, in effect, to "have its cake and eat it, too," i.e., permit broadcasters to use the spectrum for HDTV and allocate spectrum for wireless services. The additional spectrum enabled the FCC to at least in part meet the growing demand (continuing even today) for spectrum to offer advanced wireless services, such as high speed access to the Internet.

However, the trade benefits of adopting an ATSC standard are not clear. Policymakers were initially motivated to focus on the value of HDTV by the possibility of losing to Japan in a trade war. Today, after the FCC did its part by adopting the ATSC standard, European and Japanese companies are among the world's leading

manufacturers of HDTV sets. It is perhaps ironic that although the US "won" the HDTV standards war, American companies gained little: they only get royalty fees while the Europeans and Japanese captured the market to sell TV sets to consumers.

Further research: The case studies discussed in this paper illustrate several successful efforts by the FCC to promote new entrants, e.g., commercial radio, cable deregulation, DBS entry. In Starr's formulation, "change would come … slowly," but, when the Commission makes the right call the results can be truly transformative.

However, these examples may not be sufficient to establish that the decade of the 1970s marks a decisive turning point in favor of promoting new entrants at the expense of incumbents. There are as many counter examples where the FCC favored new entrants before the 1970s, such as the decision to promote commercial radio in 1928, and *Carterfone*, decided in 1968. Other efforts by the FCC to promote competitive entry (e.g., video dialtone, open video systems) may not have been as successful.[168] Additionally, though not discussed here, policies that favor incumbents have also been adopted since the 1970's.[169]

More research is needed in order to determine whether FCC decision-making falls into a pattern favoring incumbents or new entrants.

---

[168] Daniel L. Brenner, "Creating Effective Broadband Network Regulation, *Federal Communications Law Journal,* Vol. 62, #1, at 13, 32-34 (2010).

[169] *See e.g.,* Susan P. Crawford, "The Radio and the Internet," *Berkeley Tech. L.J.* 23, no. 2 (2008) at 933, 989 ("At the conclusion of the Commission's work during the summer of 2007 on the 700 MHz auctions, the FCC emerged from the brawl with negotiated arrangements that largely served incumbents' interests.").

Bibliography

Carl Shapiro and Hal R. Varian, *Information Rules* (1999)

Christopher H. Sterling, John Michael Kittross, *Stay Tuned: A History of American Broadcasting* (2002)

Daniel Brenner *et al*, *Cable Television and Other Nonbroadcast Video: Law and Policy* (2004)

Daniel L. Brenner, "Creating Effective Broadband Network Regulation, *Federal Communications Law Journal*, Vol. 62, #1, at 13, 32-34 (2010).

David Horne, *Market Oriented Spectrum Policy Evolution in the United States*, (2009)

Edward A. Comor, *Communication, Commerce, and Power: The Political Economy of America and the Direct Broadcast Satellite, 1960-2000* (1998)

Eric Klinenberg, *Fighting for Air: The Battle to Control America's Media* (2007)

Evan Kwerel, and Jonathan Levy, "The DTV Transition in the U.S.," in Martin Cave and Kyoshi Nakamura, Editors, *Digital Broadcasting: Policy and Practice in the Americas, Europe and Japan* (2006)

Florence Setzer and Jonathan Levy, *"Broadcast Television in a Multichannel Marketplace,"* OPP Working Paper Series (FCC, June 1991)

Glen O. Robinson, "The Titanic Remembered: AT&T and the Changing World of Telecommunications," 5 *Yale Journal of Regulation* 517, 520-32 (1988) *excerpted in* Thomas Krattenmaker, *Telecommunications Law and Policy* (1998).

Gregory S. Crawford, "Cable Regulation in the Satellite Era," (2006), http://www.u.arizona.edu/~gsc818/research/papers/cablereg.pdf.

Hugh R. Slotten, *Radio and Television Regulation, Broadcast Technology in the United States,* 1920-1960 (2000)

Jacques Pelkmans, "The GSM Standard: Explaining a European Success Story, *Journal of European Public Policy* (2001)

Jason Oxman, *The FCC and the Unregulation of the Internet* (OPP Working Paper, July 1999)

Joel Brinkley, *Defining Vision: The Battle for the Future of Television* (1997)

John Berresford, *"How Government Can Bring New Communications to All Americans: Six Lessons of History,"* Program on Information Resources Policy, Harvard University (2004), http://pirp.harvard.edu/pubs_pdf/berresf/berresf-p04-2.pdf..

Jonathan E. Nuechterlein and Philip J. Weiser, *Digital Crossroads: American Telecommunications Policy in the Internet Age* (2005)

Joseph Farrell and Carl Shapiro, *"Standard Setting in High Definition Television,"* Brookings Papers (1992)

Lucio Fuentelsaz *et al*, "The Evolution of mobile communications in Europe: The Transition from the second to the third generation," *Telecommunications Policy* 32 (2008)

Marc K. Landy and Martin A. Levin, "Creating Competitive Markets: The Politics of Market Design," in Marc K. Landy et al, *Creating Competitive Markets: The Politics of Regulatory Reform* (2007)

Marc Delprat and Vinod Kumar, "Second Generation Systems," in Jerry D. Gibson, editor, *The Mobile Communications Handbook* (1996).

Michael Dupagne and Peter B. Seel, *HDTV: A Global Perspective* (1998)

Michael K. Kellogg, John Thorne, and Peter W. Huber, *Federal Telecommunications Law* (1992)

N.Gandal *et al*, Standards in Wireless Networks, *Telecommunications Policy* 27 (2003)

Paul Starr, *The Creation of the Media* (2004)

Reed E. Hundt, *Statement,* Committee on Commerce, Science, and Transportation, United States Senate (February 23, 1994)

Reed Hundt, *You Say You Want a Revolution: A Story of Information Age Politics* (2000)

Robert McChesney, *Telecommunications, Mass Media, and Democracy: The Battle for Control of U.S. Broadcasting, 1928-1935* (1994)

Robert W. Crandall and Harold Furchtgott-Roth, *Cable Television: Regulation or Competition* (1996)

Roger Noll, Merton Peck, and John J. McGowan, *Economic Aspects of Television Regulation,* (1973)

Staff Report, *Policies for Regulation of Direct Broadcast Satellites* (Office of Plans and Policy, September 1980)

Stanley M. Besen and Robert W. Crandall, "The Deregulation of Cable Television," 44 *Law and Contemporary Problems* 77, 79 (1981)

Stanly M. Besen, Thomas G. Krattenmaker, A. Richard Metzger, Jr., and John R. Woodbury, *Misregulating Television* (1984)

Stuart Minor Benjamin, Douglas Gary Lichtman, Howard A. Shelanski, *Telecommunications Law and Policy (*2001)

Susan P. Crawford, "The Radio and the Internet," *Berkeley Tech. L.J.* 23, no. 2 (2008)

T.R. Reid, *The United States of Europe: the New Superpower and the End of American Supremacy (*2004)
Thomas Streeter, *Selling the Air: A Critique of the Policy of Commercial Broadcasting in the United States* (1996*)*

Walter Mossberg, "Free my Phone, *Wall Street Journal,* http://mossblog.allthingsd.com/20071021/free-my-phone

Other Recent Staff Papers

All Titles Can Be Downloaded at
http://www.fcc.gov/papers/

"Maximum Impact for Minimum Subsidy: Reverse Auctions for Universal Access in Chile and India," Irene S. Wu, FCC Staff Working Paper 2, October 2010.

"A Market-Based Approach to Establishing Licensing Rules: Licensed versus Unlicensed Use of Spectrum," Mark Bykowsky, Mark Olson, and William Sharkey, OSP Working Paper 43, February 2008

"Modeling the Efficiency of Spectrum Designated to License Use and Unlicensed Operations," Mark Bykowsky, Mark Olson, and William Sharkey, OSP Working Paper 42, February 2008.

"Enhancing Spectrum's Value via Market-Informed Congestion Etiquettes," Mark Bykowsky, Kenneth Carter, Mark Olson, and William Sharkey, OSP Working Paper 41, February 2008.

"Competition Between Cable Television and Direct Broadcast Satellite - It's More Complicated Than You Think," Andrew S. Wise and Kiran Duwadi, Media and International Bureaus, January 2005.

"The Scarcity Rationale for Regulating Traditional Broadcasting: An Idea Whose Time Has Passed," John W. Berresford, Media Bureau, March 2005.

"A Survival Analysis of Cable Networks," Keith S. Brown, Media Bureau, December 2004.

"Traits of an Independent Communications Regulator: a Search for Indicators," by Irene Wu, International Bureau, June 2004.

"The Limits of Economic Regulation: The U.S. Experience," Peyton L. Wynns, International Bureau, June 2004.